The

Song
of
Deborah

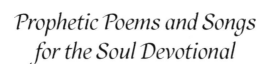

*Prophetic Poems and Songs
for the Soul Devotional*

DEBORAH CADORE

Trilogy Christian Publishers
A Wholly Owned Subsidiary of Trinity Broadcasting Network
2442 Michelle Drive
Tustin, CA 92780

For information, address Trilogy Christian Publishing
Rights Department, 2442 Michelle Drive, Tustin, CA 92780.
Trilogy Christian Publishing/TBN and colophon are trademarks of
Trinity Broadcasting Network.
For information about special discounts for bulk purchases, please
contact Trilogy Christian Publishing.
Manufactured in the United States of America

10 9 8 7 6 5 4 3 2 1
Library of Congress Cataloging-in-Publication Data is available.
ISBN 979-8-88738-774-1
ISBN 979-8-88738-775-8 (ebook)

Foreword

I met Deborah Cadore through a like-minded spiritual group. It was through this group; I saw her commitment to God and the gifts He placed in her to encourage and inspire others. She has been a blessing to my life as she has supported and offered her time and talent in assisting me with my vision in ministry.

It is the passion of Deborah to lift the spirit of others, especially you as the reader. The Holy Spirit filled songs, poems, and prayers included in this book will offer you peace, tranquility, and the encouragement to trust God, experience the love of Jesus Christ, and receive empowerment from Holy Spirit. As you read this book, let your soul be refreshed and renewed. Let each song, poem, and prayer speak to your heart and transform your daily walk with The Lord.

Because of Deborah's labor of love, may your life, those you love, and those you share this beautiful collection with be richly blessed.

-Rosemary Winbush,
Marketplace Shepherd

"I will sing to the Lord because He has dealt bountifully with me."

Psalms 13:6 AMP

Preface

In a world of uncertainty and turbulent times, I find the faith of many is being tested. This is the time we must encourage ourselves and each other in the Lord.

The Song of Deborah is a daily devotional that speaks to life's situations.

With songs, poems, and prayers inspired by the Holy Spirit, this book will provide encouragement for the soul.

No matter what you're going through, I pray that you are edified, exhorted, and comforted each day you read a passage from this book. Allow God's word to minister to you as you continue on your path of life.

I wrote this book because we have much to be thankful for despite the challenges we face on a daily basis. We are reminded each day of His grace and mercy. I pray that if you don't have a personal relationship with Jesus, that you get to know Him. And as a result, I believe that you too will have a new song to sing!

Acknowledgments

Firstly, I want to thank God for His love, His mercy, and His faithfulness! Thank You for opening doors for me that no man can shut!

To my sister and best friend Michelle: Thanks for your love and support! And for always being a voice of reason in my life. I love you always.

To my dearest daughter, Nathisa: Thanks for your honesty and your love. God blessed me with you and for that I'm grateful.

I'd like to thank my bonus kids Cornaisia and Ackeem for your love and support!

To my parents, the Rev. Elijah and Deidre Peters: Thank you for training me up in the way that I should go. Thank you for your continued prayers and for never giving up on me.

To my dear friend Minister Angel: This book would not be possible if it weren't for you and your genuine love and encouragement throughout the years! Thank you for seeing in me what I couldn't see in myself at times. You are an answer to prayer!

To my friend and mentor Prophet Andrea: Thanks for pushing me out of my comfort zone and for setting such an awesome example! You are truly an inspiration.

To my friend and business partner Elder Sheryl: Thanks

for the years of encouragement and support!

And to my dear friends and family: Thank you for being a part of my journey and helping me grow as a person.

Last but certainly not least, I'd like to thank my husband KC for his love and support. You truly helped me understand how to ride the waves of life. Thank you for teaching me fortitude. I love you!

Table of Contents

"How to Be More Like You" Song

Lord, show me how to love, in the true meaning of the word!
Teach me to sacrifice, expecting nothing in return.
Show me how to give as You've instructed me to do.
Please teach me how to be more like You, Lord.

Lord, show me how to live my life the way You want me to.
Teach me how to heed advice from those You're speaking through.
Help my life reflect You in all I say and do.
Please teach me how to be more like You, Lord.

Lord, show me how to be when things are not going my way.
Teach me how to know
When to hold my peace and pray.
Help me to forgive as You've instructed me to do.
Please teach me how to be more like You, Lord.

"And be not conformed to this world: but be ye transformed by the renewing of your mind, that ye may prove what is that good, and acceptable, and perfect, will of God."

Romans 12:2

Dear God,

We long to be more like You every day! Renew our minds with Your Word, O God. Help us to decrease in order that You can increase in our lives. Our desire is to reflect the love that You've given us to those we encounter. Help us to put aside pride and ego as these things only hinder us from being the people You've called us to be. Thank You for reminding us that Your ways are not our ways, and Your thoughts are not our thoughts. But by Your grace, we know we can represent You in a powerful way today. Take charge by Your Spirit, O God. And please forgive us for holding onto past hurts and disappointments. We believe what Your Word says about us is true. Today is a new day! We bless You and praise You.

In the blessed name of Jesus we pray,

Amen

The Refiner's Fire

He refines us like the silversmith refines silver to produce wares,
And like the goldsmith produces gold using fire and pressure.
He purifies us like metal that is put into the furnace in order that we are made fit for the Master's use. You may ask what could be the reason to have to endure such hardship
And pressure that's seemingly unbearable and even painful at times.
It boggles the mind!
Man can't fully comprehend the logic or reasoning behind such things.
There's more to life than what the eye can see.
I'm talking about spiritual things.
We are His craftsmanship, and how He's orchestrated it is that we must be transformed—That is molded and shaped in order for us to reflect His image.
Each and every day we must strive to be a "mirror image" of Christ our Savior.
Therefore, we must be stripped away from impurities and those "things"
That would easily beset us, hinder, or even destroy us.

But, if we choose to trust in Him, our creator who is attempting to refine us,
Then we can be assured that He won't allow us to perish.
For He has predestined us to be as He is, which is perfect!
Perfect meaning complete, whole, with nothing missing, and nothing broken.
Without blemish, blameless, without spot or wrinkle.
We can't do an "inkling" of this on our own, but He has shown us time and time again,
That by His grace we can face whatever trial, tribulation, temptation, condemnation, even correction, adversity, or affliction.
Knowing that we have received redemption, and justification because of the shed blood of Christ.
He is the Way, the Truth, and the Life.
Let us then count it all joy as we go through the fire knowing that God is with us!
And in the end, this produces patience, meaning endurance.
Remember that these minor afflictions aren't even worthy to be compared to the glory, That is set before us.
For we are victorious!!!
Knowing that if God is for us, who can be against us?
We are in good hands!
For we are in the hands of the Refiner.

Deborah Cadore

"And he shall sit as a refiner and purifier of silver: and he shall purify the sons of Levi, and purge them as gold and silver, that they may offer unto the LORD an offering in righteousness."
Malachi 3:3

Dear God,

Your loving hand corrects, prunes, and brings us into a place of purity. Our desire is to be Your vessel fit for Your use. Lord, mold us and shape us into Your image.

And help us not to despise Your correction because Your word says that You chasten whom You love. Like a diamond that was formed from coal has to endure extreme heat and pressure, Lord, help us to endure these tests and trials. We may not know why we go through all that we do but I pray that we hold fast to the profession of our faith without wavering. And that ultimately we allow life's challenges to draw us closer to You rather than away from You. For these light afflictions are not worthy to be compared to the eternal glory that is set before us. O God, help us remember that You've endured the cross for us, and that we will overcome by Your blood and by the word of our testimony. Knowing that You are working all things out for our good. Thank You for Your grace to make it through yet another day.

In Jesus' name we pray,

Amen

"Stress-less"

On the days I encounter stress due to things that are
seemingly beyond my reach,
Sometimes I feel less than able to be the person that I
know I can be.
It's clear to me that I'm not functioning at my best.
It's difficult for me to see my way through this series of
tests.
And oftentimes I feel stuck and unable to thrive.
It's in these moments that I must push myself to survive.
Many of us find it hard to navigate these uncertain times.
But ultimately, we must realize that we're not built to do
everything on our own.
For His word has shown us to not be anxious for
anything but in all things,
With prayer and supplication,
To Him, we can make our requests known.
Lord, help us to see that You are in control!
For You are faithful!
You are able!
You are more than capable!
So, I surmise that stress and worry cannot benefit me.
And I need not hurry to entertain these things.
I've decided to relinquish all my cares to You,

The Song of Deborah

The One who can do the impossible!
For You know what's best!
And from this day forward,
I will choose to stress less!

"Do not be anxious or worried about anything, but in everything [every circumstance and situation] by prayer and petition with thanksgiving, continue to make your [specific] requests known to God."

Philippians 4:6 AMP

Dear Heavenly Father,

Lord, You promised not to give us more than we can bear.

At times when we realize that we're carrying too much, we know that we can lay our burdens at Your feet because You care for us. For Your Word says that Your yoke is easy and Your burden is light. Each day, help us to remember what our priorities are. That we may do what we can, but relinquish to You what is out of our control. Please forgive us if we allow ourselves to get distracted at times, and teach us how to manage our time more effectively so that we're not frustrated.

Today we endeavor to lay aside all worry, as it does not benefit us, and we choose Your peace which surpasses understanding. From this day forward, I will focus on Your Word, which will not return void. Give us wisdom regarding making decisions as well as taking on new assignments and commitments, even as it pertains to utilizing our time and money. Thank You for leading us and guiding by Your Spirit.

In Jesus' name,

Amen

Have Faith

*More often than not, I forget the things You've brought
me through.*

*There is no one greater than You, and no one can do
what only YOU can do!*

*I wish it was that simple. Just to trust and obey as the
song says,*

*To not be led by what I see, by my emotions, or by what's
going on around me.*

But still and all, I've decided to walk by faith!

It was by faith that I received You as my Lord and King,

*It is by faith that I trust You along the journey to my
destiny.*

*It is by faith that I know not to worry and trust You as
my Jehovah Jireh,*

Which means You are my provider!

It is by faith that I have made it this far.

For You are faithful!

Faith works by love.

And so I will have faith in who You are!

"Now faith is the substance of things hoped for, the evidence of things not seen."
Hebrews 11:1 KJV

Dear God,

You are the author and the finisher of our faith! Help us to trust in You even when times get rough, knowing that Your Word is true! And even when our faith is weak, we thank You for being faithful! Thank You for showing us that You are with us every step of the way! Whether we are on the mountain or in the valley, You are still God! Forgive us for allowing our situations to sometimes cause us to forget that You are greater than our circumstances. Let us go forward with the assurance that even when life seems uncertain, You never change! Help us to guard our hearts today and every day,

and to seek You in all that we do. You are our banner! For we know that through You we have the victory!

It is in Jesus' name we pray,

Amen

A Grateful Heart

God, I'm so grateful for who YOU are!

You are the truest, most assured, most loving One that I know by far!

You are everywhere I go!

You've never left me alone.

You, God, are always in control.

You are able!

You are willing to do exceedingly abundantly above all that I could ask or think.

And so, I'm grateful!

I thank You, and I praise You!

For You are good, You are lovely, You are faithful!

Even at my lowest, I can look to You, for You are my helper and my friend.

You make all things new!

And there is no end to Your love.

Forgive me for putting other things above You.

Thank You for loving me despite my flaws!

For this cause I'm grateful!

Sincerely,

A grateful heart

"In everything give thanks: for this is the will of God in Christ Jesus concerning you."

1 Thessalonians 5:18 KJV

Deborah Cadore

Gracious Father,

We come into Your gates with thanksgiving, and into Your courts with praise today. Lord, no matter what today brings, we know that this is the day that You have made, and so we will endeavor to rejoice and be glad in it. Help us today to choose to focus on Your goodness despite the negative things that may be going on around us. Teach us to number our days, O God. Thank You for surrounding us with Your presence! And at times when we feel like complaining, help us to remember that we have so much to be grateful for. Let us be determined to delight ourselves in You every day. We praise You for who You are, for You are so good! Have Your way in and through us today.

It is in Your matchless name we pray,

Amen

Lead Me and I Will Follow

He leads me.

He guides me.

He provides for me entirely.

He is my shepherd,

My helper, and my provider.

He leads me in the paths of righteousness for His name's
sake.

For He promised to make my crooked paths straight.

I will choose to wait on You for the answer, for direction,
and for clarity.

Help me, Lord, to silence the noise around me

So that I can hear Your voice more clearly.

For it is Your still small voice that I need most dearly.

"In all thy ways acknowledge him, and he shall direct thy paths."

Proverbs 3:6

Dear Lord,

Thank You for leading us as a shepherd leads his sheep. Your word says that Your sheep hear Your voice, and another's they will not follow. Help us to silence the noise around us so that we can hear You more clearly. Open the eyes of our understanding, O God, and remove distractions and any blockages that are hindering us from going from faith to faith and glory to glory. At times when we need direction, remind us that You are as close as the mere mention of Your name. Please take confusion from the midst of us, and allow us not to get frustrated but wait patiently on You. We ask for Your guidance today.

Amen

A Song of Praise

I will shout from here to heaven singing songs of joyful
praise
For my God is able,
And He is faithful in all His ways!
He's my comforter and friend.
And His love will never end.
I will praise Him forever more!

I will sing hallelujah
For He is good!
Oh, He is good!
And above Him, there's no other
For He is good,
Yes, He is good.
There will never be another
For He is good,
Yes, He is good,
I will praise Him forevermore.

*"I will praise thee, O LORD, among the people:
and I will sing praises unto thee
among the nations."*

Psalm 57:9

Blessed Father,

Let us remember to bless You at all times even despite the negative circumstances that we may experience. Thank You for yet another day that You have made. Help us to cast our cares on You. We choose to meditate on Your goodness. Thank You that Your grace is sufficient for us today. You said in Your Word that goodness and mercy will follow us all the days of our lives, so let us walk by faith today and not by sight.

Let all that we do from this day forward be for Your glory. Thank You for blessing the works of our hands.

We will not fail to give You all the glory, honor, and praise.

Amen

Purify My Heart, Lord

*Lord, create in me a clean heart, O Lord, and renew a
right spirit within me.*

Help me to see the error of my ways.

*Lord, You are the potter and I am the clay; mold me into
Your image each and every day.*

Make my days lead to You and Your Word.

For Your Word is Love.

Your Word is true.

*Your Word is a lamp unto my feet and a light unto my
path.*

Alas, I will not despise Your reproof,

But I will choose to trust in You.

Help all that I say and do,

Reflect YOU in me.

Be my source.

Be my strength.

Be my guide.

For You are forever lovely.

You are forever kind!

You are faithful!

*And Your grace is more than able to keep me even in the
midst of uncertainty.*

Despite the heartache and pain, You still reign!

And I will worship You in all that I say and do,
That my character may be a true representation of You.
Letting go of offense in my own strength is not easy to
do,
But with You all things are possible!
You can do a work in me that is unimaginable and
unexplainable.
Transform me into Your image today.
Purify my heart, O Lord, and renew a right spirit within
me, I pray.

Deborah Cadore

"*Create in me a clean heart, O God; and renew a right spirit within me.*"

Psalm 51:10

45

Father God,

Let the words of our mouths and the meditations of our hearts be acceptable in Your sight! Help us to stop being so critical of others, but rather speak the truth in love.

May we be mindful of what comes out of our mouths, and when we miss it, let us be quick to repent. Let us endeavor to seek You moment by moment and to desire Your presence above all. And when our flesh rises up, remind us that death and life are in the power of the tongue, that we may speak your word in every situation.

Sanctify our hearts, O Lord, and remove anything that is not like You,

That we may be led by Your Spirit and not be led by our emotions,

So that You may be glorified in us and through us.

In Jesus' name,

Amen

I Am Healed!

I know You are able, and more than capable to do the
impossible.

Even at times when my faith has not been great;
You never change.

You're the same, yesterday and today.

Open the eyes of my understanding, I pray.

I ask myself if I truly believe that You can heal me.

Yes, Lord, I believe!!!

So I will cry out to thee and say...

That even in my dismay, You still reign!

God, I will choose not to focus on what I see but to focus
on You, for Your Word is true!

You are my strength!

And You are my shield!

You are my Jehovah Rapha!

And by Your stripes, I'm healed!

I will continue to praise You, my King!

For You are Jehovah Rapha, the Lord that heals me!

I declare that healing is my portion!

I decree that I have been set free!

*"Who his own self bare our sins in his own body
on the tree, that we, being dead to sins, should live
unto righteousness: by whose stripes
ye were healed."*

1 Peter 2:24 KJV

Gracious Heavenly Father,

We believe that You are our healer! Healing is our portion!

You are able to do exceedingly abundantly above all that we can ask or think!

And Your word is true! You never change! You are the same, yesterday, today, and forever! We will stand on Your Word and trust in Your promises, for they are yes and amen! For You are our deliverer! You are our savior! And even when we feel like our world is closing in all around us, You remind us that Your presence is always there.

We come out of agreement with fear and doubt.

And today we speak to the mountain and say, "Be removed!" That is, the mountain of fear, anxiety, sickness, poverty, grief, loneliness, and anything that would keep us bound.

O God, You who knew us before we were formed in the womb,

Nothing has taken You by surprise. You are in complete control!

And so we bless You and we praise You, for You are good!

You have the final say! Thank You for the victory!

Lord, let Your glory shine within us today we pray!

Amen

A Song of Gladness

Rejoice and be glad!
For God is good!
He makes my crooked paths straight.
His wisdom is infinite,
And His mercy is great.
His love is endless!
He is my reason to sing.
He has given me beauty for my ashes!
For He is doing a new thing!
He has caused me to triumph!
And if God be for me,
Who can be against me?
There is nothing that my God cannot do!
He has made me glad!
In His presence my joy is plentiful!

"For thou, LORD, hast made me glad through thy work: I will triumph in the works of thy hands."

Psalm 92:4 KJV

Dear Lord,

Thank You for who You are. You are our reason to sing! Even in times of war, famine, and civil unrest, we know we can trust in You! You have brought us through and continue to keep us. Help us to realize that even in the midst of the storms of life, You continue to surround us with Your love, and that Your presence is always with us. For in Your presence is the fullness of joy! We know that the joy You give is our strength. Today we choose to walk in gladness and not allow anything to steal our joy! For You, O Lord, can take what the Enemy meant for evil, and turn it around for our good! In You, we have the victory! You have caused us to triumph! Have Your way today!

In Your name,

Amen

Beauty for Ashes

Let us not take for granted the beauty that is everywhere
even in our despair.
For if we choose to cast our cares on Him,
He will show us that His presence is always there.
It is in our darkest hours that His light can be seen.
Don't be afraid, because it is in these moments
That these things are beautifully constructed into being.
Because it is out of ashes that He creates beauty.
And likewise, out of the dust He created us.

"To appoint unto them that mourn in Zion, to give unto them beauty for ashes, the oil of joy for mourning, the garment of praise for the spirit of heaviness; that they might be called trees of righteousness, the planting of the LORD, that he might be glorified."

Isaiah 61:3 KJV

Deborah Cadore

Almighty God,

We bless You this day for taking the things in our lives that are not pretty and creating a better us. For You said in Your Word that all things work together for the good of them that love You and are called according to Your purpose. Thank You for doing a new thing in us, O God. Restore us as well as our health, our relationships, finances, and even our joy! Renew hope within us, that we may experience your shalom, and let us not take Your blessings for granted. Lead us today, as You are our Shepherd. Empower us by Your Spirit to live according to Your will. In the matchless name of Jesus we pray,

Amen

Don't Be Overwhelmed

Have you ever felt overwhelmed?
I used to have panic attacks, with fear gripping me at the
helm.
I would worry often
And carried much inside
Like I had the weight of the world on my shoulders,
And there was no place to hide.
I became everything to everybody, except who was
supposed to take care of me?
My heart was overwhelmed and overloaded with anxiety.
Then one day I had an epiphany.
Why not allow God to take control of my situation
without having any reservations?
He promised that He would not give me more than I can
bear
And I've been carrying way too much on my shoulders.
God says, "Release those things to Me without
hesitation!
When you are weak, I Am strong!
How long will you keep trying to be the one and only
solution to a thing?
When all you need to do is to seek Me first, and all these
'things' will be handled accordingly.

I can guide and lead you!
I can show you what to do and what not to do.
If you choose to allow Me,
I can do the impossible!
Do not be discouraged or dismayed, "
Sayeth the Spirit of Grace.

"From the end of the earth will I cry unto thee,
When my heart is overwhelmed: Lead me to the
rock that is higher than I."

Psalm 61:2 KJV

Dear Gracious Father,

Many times, we find ourselves at a loss because we try to do things in our own strength. Thank You, Lord, for lovingly reminding us that we humans are limited, but You, O God, are limitless! And when we find ourselves getting frustrated at times, and our hearts are overwhelmed, You said that You would lead us to the rock that is higher than us. Father, You are our solid foundation. We can stand on Your Word, for it is sure and it never fails. Help us to not lose courage when we face adversity, knowing that You are greater than any trial that we face. In You, O God, we can find rest!

We lay our cares on You today, and in turn, we receive Your peace.

In the name above every name,

Amen

Greater Is He Song

Greater is He that's in me than He that's in the world.
I could do all things through Christ,
Because He strengthens me.
I am more than a conqueror.
No weapon formed against me shall prosper!
Oh, greater is He
That's in me!

When trials and temptations are mounting
He has given me the authority
To speak to the mountain
Satan is defeated
And we have the victory!
Greater is He
That's in me!

"Ye are of God, little children, and have overcome them: because greater is he that is in you, than he that is in the world."

1 John 4:4 KJV

Deborah Cadore

Father,

Thank You for empowering us by Your Spirit to be overcomers! You are greater than any circumstance or situation. Today we choose to allow Your light to shine within us even in the darkest moments, for we know that we can do all things through Christ who strengthens us! Have Your way in and through us today, O God, and use us as Your vessels. And when we encounter obstacles, give us Your wisdom and understanding. Thank You for Your grace which is sufficient for us! Our hearts are surrendered to Your leading. Show Yourself mighty on our behalf today. We declare that we have the victory!

In Jesus' name we pray,

Amen

No Greater Love

*There is no greater love than the One who gave His Son
to die for me.*

*He created me and felt it not robbery to go to Hell and
back in order for me to be free.*

His love never fades
It never changes
It's unconditional
And never goes through phases
His love never fails
And even when those close to me at times disappoint me,
His love continues to surround me
It truly confounds me
Because I can do no "thing" to earn His love,
There is nothing I can do to lose it.
Nothing remotely resembles it (His love)
Nothing can replace it.
It just is….
For God is love
And God says, "Be still and know,
That I Am your first love.
And I will never let you go!"

"Greater love hath no man than this, that a man lay down his life for his friends."

John 15:13 KJV

Dear God,

Thank You for loving us so much that You gave Your Son to die in order that we may have eternal life with You! And even when we feel like we are not loved, You remind us that there is no greater love than this, for someone to lay down their life for their friends. You, O God, have called us Your friend! We can come to You for wisdom, comfort, healing, provision, and for anything that we need. You said for us to ask and we shall receive! Father, we ask that Your love transform our hearts to love the way we should love. For You said to love You with all of our hearts and minds, and to love our neighbor as we love ourselves. Some of us need You, O God, to reveal to us what true love is! For it is as we get to know who You are that we will know love, for You, God, are love! And You love us despite our flaws. We receive Your love today. We love You and we praise You!

It is in Your Son's name we pray,

Amen

Blessed

Oftentimes I encounter someone in need
Whether they need food to feed themselves or their
families or whether they just need encouragement to
"keep on keeping on" despite any THING.
I cast no judgment because, under different
circumstances, that could be me.
My heart goes out to the desolate, to those that feel as
though they have nothing left, and to those just needing
a second chance at life.
I wish at times that there was more that I could do.
That is when I pray to the God of the Breakthrough!
For He so loved the world that He gave us His Son
And so I choose to give, to be a blessing to someone in
need.
It's better to give than to receive.
Some may give out of abundance, and others give what
they can.
But to truly live and not just simply exist in this world,
It means to be a helping hand.
And it starts with you and me,
To be God's hands and feet.
It may mean to give not just monetarily,
But of my time and talent willingly

To reach out and help someone even if I'm going through
the very same thing!
That is what it means to sow seeds that you want to reap.
The Bible says we reap what we sow,
So why not sow good seeds?
And at times when I've been faced with adversity,
His grace has been sufficient for me.
He is our provider and will supply all our needs.
We are blessed to be a blessing.

Deborah Cadore

"Blessed and worthy of praise be the God and Father of our Lord Jesus Christ, who has blessed us with every spiritual blessing in the heavenly realms in Christ."

Ephesians 1:3 AMP

Dear Blessed Father,

It is because of You that we can say that we are blessed! Thank You for blessing us with a new day! For this is the day that the Lord has made, and we will rejoice and be glad in it! We thank You for our families, our loved ones, and the people whom You have brought into our lives. Help us to count our blessings each and every day and not take the things that You've given us for granted. We thank You for your peace that surpasses all understanding. May we grow closer to You as we take time to meditate on Your goodness that can be seen throughout our lives. Let us remember that we are blessed to be a blessing, and that it is more blessed to give than to receive. Show us the opportunities in which we can be a blessing to someone else. Help us to be Your hands and feet in this journey called life.

In the name of Jesus,

Amen

"The Principal Thing"

Wisdom is the principal thing,
And in all things, get understanding.
Wisdom dwells with prudence, meaning they go hand in hand.
For knowledge without understanding is like having a recipe without the key ingredient.
We need the wisdom of God in order to function in this life effectively,
And to make decisions that can ultimately affect us and our families.
Even our destiny.
The wisdom of God is infinite,
And is of more benefit than diamonds and rubies.
It is the most extravagant.
It can keep you from destructive patterns and behaviors.
It will lead you to reverence our Lord and Savior.
It can transform how you think,
And teach you when and how to speak.
For it is the principal thing.

"I, [godly] wisdom, reside with prudence [good judgment, moral courage, and astute common sense], And I find knowledge and discretion."

Proverbs 8:12 AMP

Dear God,

We pray for wisdom today. Help us to make the right decisions not only for us but for those we are responsible for.

Give us discernment as we deal with people every day. Help us to avoid toxic patterns and cycles, and please forgive us for not seeking You first in all the areas of our lives. Open the eyes of our understanding today.

Thank You, O Lord, for leading and guiding us by Your Spirit.

In Your name,

Amen

My Safe Place

You are my strong tower!
I run into You and I'm safe!
For You, O Lord, are my shelter!
You hide me under the shadow of Your wings.
You show me great and mighty things.
You pour Your love over me
And heal me from sickness and disease.
You even expose those hidden areas deep within me
That would try to hinder me from my destiny.
You are my refuge and my fortress!
In You will I trust!
I will not fear
For You are with me.
You correct me
You protect me
You comfort me
You are my place of safety.

"For thou hast been a shelter for me, and a strong tower from the enemy."

Psalm 61:3

Dear Lord,

Our desire is to continually dwell in Your secret place!

We know that in You we find safety! Your love surrounds us! And in Your presence, we find peace even amid uncertainty. Hide us under the shadow of Your wings and keep us, O God.

Thank You for helping us see that You are greater and stronger than our adversities. Please keep us close to You so that we may have a deeper knowledge of who You are!

Manifest Yourself in us like never before today. We give You permission to work through us today.

You are our comforter and friend, and You are close as the mere mention of Your name. Help us to trust You more and more each day.

In Your name we pray,

Amen

I Know Who I Am

For years I battled with identifying who I truly am.
I knew whom I aspired to be and used to often imitate
those whom I've admired, you see.
I would say things like, "I wish I could be like this
person."
But what I really meant was that I wasn't happy with
being me.
Not realizing at a young age that when God created me,
He made me unique.
And He gave me all that I need, including my
personality.
Ultimately, the person to admire is Jesus Christ.
For it is He who gave me my identity.
It was by the adoption into His family that I can be
called a child of the King.
And as such, He endowed me with gifts, talents, and
spiritual things.
In Him, I have an inheritance.
In Him, I am accepted.
In Him, I am loved.
In Him, I am seated in heavenly places.

*"But ye are a chosen generation, a royal
priesthood, an holy nation, a peculiar people; that
ye should shew forth the praises of him who hath
called you out of darkness into his marvelous light."*

1 Peter 2:9 KJV

Dear Father,

Thank You for reminding us of who we are! Many of us have thought of ourselves as being less than what Your Word says about us. Help us to Go to believe the lies of the Enemy that would try to get us to doubt who we are. You have created us to do great things! In You, we have our identity! You created us in Your image. We are Your beloved and no one can pluck us out of Your hand! No one can separate us from Your love!

Let us go forward today knowing that we are Your children, that You are our Father, and that we can come boldly to Your throne and cry out to You!!

Amen

I Will Focus on You

Your word says to fear not,
So why should I be afraid?
Rather I choose to believe.
For is not fear the opposite of faith?

And why should I wallow in self-pity and shame,
If I trust in Your name
For You said I'm forgiven
And old things are passed away.

Why do I seemingly feel stuck like I'm in a rut,
Unable to rise to the level I desire to achieve?
Many times I get distracted,
Focusing on all the wrong things.

Dear child,
You can count on Me!
My word will never change.
I always remain the same.

Don't lose sight of the vision,
By focusing on the obstacles you see.
But rather choose to focus on Me.

For I know the plans I have for you,
And they are plans to prosper you and not to harm you,
Plans to make you into whom you are destined to be.

Deborah Cadore

Make me understand the way of Your precepts, So that I will meditate (focus my thoughts) on Your wonderful works.

Psalms 119:27 AMP

Dear Gracious Heavenly Father,

Help us to focus on You, O God, and not our problems. You alone are bigger than any situation or circumstance! We seek You today for wisdom and understanding, and we propose to silence the noise around us so that we can hear You more clearly. We endeavor to make You a priority; forgive us when we get distracted. And in moments that we fall short, thank You for being our glory and the lifter up of our heads. We know that You are with us every step of the way. Thank You for loving us unconditionally.

We honor and praise You!

Amen

Never Left Me Alone

God, You said that You would never leave me nor forsake
me!
When all my friends and loved ones are gone
Lord, You remain.
Your love remains the same.
You have and continue to pursue me
With your love which is unfailing and never-ending
For You are never changing
And Your presence is always with me.
You're my helper
My friend
My soon-coming King
At times of adversity, I will run to You,
The One who will never reject me
And under Your wings I find safety.
At times when I feel like I am on my own,
You remind me that I'm never alone,
And that You are with me.

"Let your character [your moral essence, your inner nature] be free from the love of money [shun greed—be financially ethical], being content with what you have; for He has said, "I WILL NEVER [under any circumstances] DESERT YOU [nor give you up nor leave you without support, nor will I in any degree leave you helpless], NOR WILL I FORSAKE or LET YOU DOWN or RELAX MY HOLD ON YOU [assuredly not]!"

Hebrews 13:5 AMP

Dear God,

Thank You for never leaving us or forsaking us! We are never alone!

In You, we have all that we need! When we face difficulties, You lovingly remind us that we are Your masterpiece, and with Your grace, we know we can represent Your kingdom in a powerful way. Take charge by Your Spirit today, that we may feel Your presence as we function throughout the day. Lead us in the paths of righteousness, O Lord, despite the busyness of the day. Help us to hear Your still small voice. We know that You are in control no matter what comes our way. Thank You for Your peace today!

In the name of Jesus, we pray.

Amen

In Your Presence

The joy of the Lord is my strength!
He makes me glad in so many ways.
I choose to delight myself in Him.
He is my rock and my refuge.
He has taken my tears and turned them into morning
dew.
He makes all things new.
O Lord, all good things come from You!
In Your presence is the fullness of my joy!

"Thou wilt shew me the path of life: In thy presence is fulness of joy; At thy right hand there are pleasures for evermore."

Psalms 16:11 KJV

Deborah Cadore

Dear Father,

We come into Your gates with thanksgiving and into Your courts with praise today, O God. As we enter into Your presence, we are filled with joy and gladness. It is in Your presence that we find peace even in the midst of any storm that we may face. Where would we be without Your presence? Our desire is to dwell with You in Your secret place. Give us our daily bread today, Father, and as we go about our routines, help us to be reminded of Your grace and mercy. Also, let us show grace and mercy to those whom we come into contact with, that we may be a reflection of who You are!

We thank You and we praise You.

Amen

Deliverance Is My Portion

He has healed my broken heart.

He has made me whole.

He has delivered me from my destruction.

He has restored my soul.

Deliverance is my portion.

He has opened the eyes of my understanding.

And by His blood,

I've been made free.

For whom He sets free

Is free indeed!

"The LORD is near to those who have a broken heart, and saves such as have a contrite spirit."

Psalms 34:18 NKJV

Father God,

Thank You for enduring the cross so that we can be free from the bondage of sin. You would desire that we have Your Shalom, that is Your peace! We know You are our healer and our deliverer. You are able to work all things out for our good. Nothing is impossible for You! Help us to allow You to heal the broken areas of our hearts. We desire to no longer be chained to our past. Help us to forgive as You have forgiven us. This also includes forgiving ourselves. Today we lay our burdens at Your feet. You, O God, are our deliverer and our portion forever! We receive our healing and deliverance now!

Amen

Your Comforter

I the Lord Am your comforter and friend.

I will be with you even until the end of time.

For I Am yours and you are Mine.

And I will uphold you with My righteous right hand.

My love will never end.

And I will be with you to help you navigate the waters of life.

Release all your burdens to Me.

And take My yoke upon you.

For it is light and easy.

You can trust in Me.

For I Am all you need.

Whether you are going through a season of pain or grief.

Hold onto your belief that I will see you through.

There is no limit to what I can do.

Sincerely,

Your Comforter

"But the Helper (Comforter, Advocate, Intercessor—Counselor, Strengthener, Standby), the Holy Spirit, whom the Father will send in My name [in My place, to represent Me and act on My behalf], He will teach you all things. And He will help you remember everything that I have told you."

John 14:26 AMP

Dear Father,

You are our comforter and a friend that sticks closer than a brother. We are grateful to be able to come to You when we are hurting and You wrap Your loving arms around us. Despite whatever condition we are in, or whatever challenges we face, we know that You are our healer. You are the God of restoration! We look to You today for Your peace that surpasses all understanding. Help us to guard our hearts and minds. For You are able to keep us from falling! Thank You for Your angels that are encamped around us and our families. We call upon Your name, for it is a strong tower! We can run into it and be saved.

We lay our burdens at Your feet! And we thank You in advance for meeting us at the point of our needs.

It is in the matchless name of Jesus we pray,

Amen

All I Need

When I was young I would find myself running into
shady situations.

As I got older, I seemed to run away from the slightest
inclination of pain and sorrow.

I've been hurt enough times to know,
How to walk away today, for the sake of a better
tomorrow.

Ultimately I developed a trend of isolation rather than
community.

And solid relationships became few and far between.

But one day I had a dream.

I encountered someone who cared for me.

He sustained me and provided for my needs.

He looked beyond my flaws and insecurities.

He even knew everything about me!

And at that moment I knew I was never alone.

Even on days when I thought I was on my own.

Now when times get rough or when everything around
me seemingly falls apart,

I know to whom I will run to.

My God is the One who holds the key to my heart.

He will never leave me undone.

For the Word says that He who began a good work in me

will finish it.-,

And the grace He gives me is more than sufficient.

He leads me into the paths of righteousness because
that's who He is.

He taught me how to love, how to trust, and how to
forgive.

Most importantly,

He taught me how to live.

And He is all I need.

"By his divine power, God has given us everything we need for living a godly life. We have received all of this by coming to know him, the one who called us to himself by means of his marvelous glory and excellence."

2 Peter 1:3 NLT

Dear Almighty God,

In You, we have all that we need. Therefore, we should not fret about our tomorrows because we know that You are faithful! We thank You for providing us with grace for today. No matter what we encounter we know that You are in control, and You promised to provide for our needs according to Your riches and glory. Our hope is in You! There is nothing that's impossible for You. We know that You are working things out for our good! As we go about our day today, we ask for Your Spirit to lead and guide us. We thank You for comforting us when we need it, for we know that our help comes from You!

Let Your glory shine within us today.

In Jesus' name,

Amen

The Battle Is the Lord's

The battle is not yours; it is the Lord's.

Who is this King of glory?

It is the Lord.

He is strong and mighty!

He triumphs over His enemies.

He makes a show over them.

There is no one greater.

No one stronger.

Take heart, for He is all powerful,

All-Knowing,

He's altogether wonderful.

And His name is the highest above every name.

He has no rival

He has no equal

He is the King that reigns.

He is the same yesterday, today, and forever.

He never changes.

He never slumbers.

And He never sleeps.

Take heed that He is the one true risen king.

He's never lost a battle.

And in Him, we have the victory!

*"And he said, Hearken ye, all Judah, and
ye inhabitants of Jerusalem, and thou king
Jehoshaphat, Thus saith the LORD unto you, Be
not afraid nor dismayed by reason of this great
multitude; for the battle is not yours, but God's."*

2 Chronicles 20:15 KJV

Deborah Cadore

Dear Father,

Despite the battles that we face, we know that in You we are victorious. You, O God, never fail! For You are our banner, our refuge, and our strength. You are our strong tower! You are our rear guard! You are the Mighty God! You, the God of angel armies! Nothing is impossible with You! Thank You for showing us time and time again that You are for us, even when we ourselves feel outnumbered. And if you be for us, then who can be against us? We will trust in You, O God! And as we encounter trials and tribulations, we will rest in the fact that the battle has been already won! We stand in agreement with Your word, and we pray from a place of victory knowing that Satan is defeated! Have Your way in us today. We give You all the praise and the glory!

Amen

Be Courageous

They say courage is not the absence of fear, but rather
acting despite fear.
I believe courage is the result of purpose.
I was created for good works and that's God's purpose
and plan for me.
And as I fulfill my purpose,
I, therefore, have Christ's backing.
So I refuse to let fear hinder me!
It is time to see myself the way God sees me!
For greater is He that's in me.
And as a person thinks in their heart, so is he.
That is the reality!
You can take courage knowing that
God's word can't return to Him void. That is a certainty.

"Have not I commanded thee? Be strong and of a good courage; be not afraid, neither be thou dismayed: for the LORD thy God is with thee whithersoever thou goest."

Joshua 1:9 KJV

Dear Lord,

So often in Your Word, we are told not to fear or be discouraged. With You by our side, of whom should we be afraid? You are our banner, protector, strength, and shield.

Today we come out of agreement with fear! You have not given us a spirit of fear but of love, power, and a sound mind! Lord, help us not to cast away our confidence but rather overcome negative thoughts that would try to hinder us, that we may step out in faith and do what it is that You purposed us to do. Give us the strength to withstand adversity. Thank You for Your Spirit that empowers us to do great things! We can be courageous because we know that You are there. You promised to be with us in trouble, so we stand on Your promises today!

In Your name,

Amen

No More Shame

When mistakes are made,
Sometimes shame is a lasting effect.
We may tend to blame ourselves
Or even live with regret.
Let us never forget God's grace,
And His mercy, that renews every morning.
It is sufficient for what we need.
And as we reflect on the deeds that we've done,
Let us also remember the blood of His Son,
That was shed for us and redeemed us from sin.
No longer are we bound by shame or disgrace
When we can walk in freedom and liberty,
That we received by God's grace.

"For the Scripture says, Whoever believes on Him will not be put to shame."
Romans 10:11 NKJVX

Dear Lord,

Thank You that we no longer have to carry guilt and shame because of the hurt from our past. You bore it all on the cross! In You we are blameless! We don't have to carry guilt and shame. Yesterday is gone and today is a new day. Father, help us to see ourselves the way You see us. Transform our hearts and minds so they are in alignment with Your Word. Let us remember that we are still a work in progress, for it is in our weakness that Your strength is made perfect. We believe Your Word that You who began a good work in us will also complete it! We surrender ourselves to You today and ask for the grace to overcome anything that would try to hinder us from being the people whom You have created us to be. Thank You for Your joy and Your peace today.

In Your name,

Amen

Be Still and Know

To be still is to be confident that You, O Lord, are in control.

It is to know that whatever the situation,
You are with me and love me without any reservation.
I will trust in You without any hesitation.
Jesus, You are the rock of my salvation.
To be still is to rest with the assurance that after I've done all that I can,
I will choose to stand upon Your promises.
For Your Word is yes and amen!
God says,
Be still and know that I Am God!
I Am He who was and is to come.
I am the Holy One,
The One True Living God.
Be still and know that I am with you wherever you go,
And that you are not alone.
Be still and know!

"Be still, and know that I am God; I will be exalted among the nations, I will be exalted in the earth!"
Psalms 46:10 NKJV

Dear Lord,

You are high and lifted up! There is no name above Your name! We thank You for this day. Despite the challenges we may encounter, we know we can trust You! Let us not be anxious about anything but let us seek You daily, for You hold us in the palm of Your hand. In You we find safety. In You we find rest. In You, we have life and life more abundantly. At times when we've done all that we can, may we be still and know that You love us and are working all things out for our good. We know that You have our best interest at heart. We ask that You guide us today and we thank You for Your peace that surpasses all understanding.

In Your name,

Amen

Let It Go

Do you find it hard to let go of offense?

What do you do when someone deeply disappoints you?

Well, for me, I used to create barriers instead of setting healthy boundaries,

At times I would isolate and engage in other proclivities.

While for some it makes sense to pretend like nothing ever fazes them.

All the while finding ways to release their frustration.

Unable to resist overwhelming temptation.

But the truth is, when we let go of the offense and forgive,

That's when our healing truly begins.

For we can be angry but still choose not to sin.

In Christ, we are more than conquerors.

He will fight our battles!

In Him, we have victory!

*"And be kind to one another, tenderhearted,
forgiving one another, even as
God in Christ forgave you."*
Ephesians 4:32 NKJV

Heavenly Father,

We choose to let go of past hurt that has kept us back from being the person You have called us to be. We forgive those who have offended us and we leave it at the foot of the cross. Help us to see if there is anything in us that we are holding onto that we need to let go of, and create in us a clean heart. We choose to take hold of Your joy, Your love, and Your peace today, and receive your healing and restoration. In You, we are made free! We are forgiven! Thank You, Father, for reminding us that old things are passed away and all things have been made new! Order our steps today, we pray.

Amen

My Provider

You are my provider!

All I need is in You.

Help me to seek You first in all that I do,
And please forgive me for missing it at times,
And show me the areas where I need your light to shine.
Even as it pertains to my finances,
Lord, grant me wisdom and knowledge to avoid negative
situations and circumstances
But rather I will call upon You!
For Your Word says that in doing so
You will answer me
And show me great and mighty things.
Thank You for all that You've done for me.
You are faithful!
You are my everything!
I will trust You.
You are able to do the impossible
For Your name is Jehovah Jireh
And You are my provider.

"And Abraham called the name of the place, The-LORD-Will-Provide; as it is said to this day, In the Mount of the LORD it shall be provided."

Genesis 22:14 NKJV

Dear Gracious Heavenly Father,

Thank You for being our provider! For Your word says that You will supply all our needs according to Your riches in glory! Your love for us is unfathomable! We need not worry for tomorrow because as You've taken care of even the sparrow, how much more will You take care of us, Your children?

And as we go about our day, O God, let us take the time to remember You and Your goodness! You are faithful! You are our present help! And You're as close as the mere mention of Your name! What a mighty God we serve! There is nothing too hard for You!

So today we cast our cares on You! We know You will show Yourself mighty on our behalf!

It is in Jesus' name we pray,

Amen

His Ambassador

We are to be His (God's) ambassadors here on earth.

What does the word "ambassador" mean?

For what it's worth,

It means that when people look at us,

It is His reflection that should be seen.

It means our lives should represent Him,

In all that we say and do;

Despite any situation,

And no matter what we are going through.

It means that when we encounter a challenge,

That by His grace we will rise above it.

For remember, we are in this world, but we're not of it.

And because His Spirit lives within us,

We shall endeavor to allow His light to shine through us,

That His love may be demonstrated by us.

Therefore, let us show love to one another.

For in doing so,

This is how the world will know us.

"So we are ambassadors for Christ, as though God were making His appeal through us; we [as Christ's representatives] plead with you on behalf of Christ to be reconciled to God."

2 Corinthians 5:20 AMP

Deborah Cadore

Gracious Heavenly Father,

Open our hearts and minds so that we can see our circumstances and situations differently, that we are led by Your Spirit and not our flesh.

We will trust in You and not lean not unto our own understanding! We're so grateful that You have chosen us to be Your sons and daughters! May we represent Your kingdom in a powerful way! And please forgive us when we fail to remember that we can't do this in our own strength and that we need You every step of the way. For in You we live and move and have our being! You are the air that we breathe! And even when we go through trials, we know that You can use them to draw us closer to You!

We ask for wisdom today, Father. May the words of our mouths and the meditations of our hearts be acceptable in Your sight, that we may lead people to You!

Amen

9 798887 387741